Nora Gracie Foster Presents

Bruno's Big Feelings

Bruno's Big Feelings
© 2025 Nora Gracie Foster. All rights reserved.

No part of this publication may be reproduced, distributed, or transmitted in any form or by any means, including photocopying, recording, or other electronic or mechanical methods, without the prior written permission of the publisher, except in the case of brief quotations embodied in critical reviews and certain other noncommercial uses permitted by copyright law.

First Edition: 2025
Designed by Stefania Grieco
Published by Stefania Grieco
Paperback ISBN: 978-1-998430-30-7
Hard Cover ISBN: 978-1-998430-31-4
eBook ISBN: 978-1-998430-29-1

Bruno's
Best Friend Is...

....

(This Story Was Made Just for...)

Write your name or draw a picture of you and Bruno here!

Bruno sits on the soft rug with green blocks.

"Look, Floppy, a **big tower**," said Bruno.

Mama Bear smiles from the chair

by the sunny window.

Floppy hops close and tilts his head.

"It is tall," said Floppy.

Papa Bear stands near the shelf

and watches Bruno

with a warm smile.

Bruno adds a red block on top.

The tower wobbles in the bright light.

Mama Bear says,

"**Careful**, my little bear,"

while watching from her chair.

The tower falls with a loud clack.

Bruno's eyes grow wide, and his paws curl.

"**No!**" said Bruno,

staring at the fallen blocks.

Floppy steps back and holds his scarf.

"It is okay," said Floppy.

Bruno lets out a **roar**

that shakes the

green and red blocks.

Papa Bear kneels beside Bruno.

"Your **roar** is big," said Papa Bear.

Bruno looks at the floor and **frowns**

while his paws press into the rug.

Mama Bear walks over with calm steps.

"Let us **help you**," said Mama Bear.

Bruno's paws still hold tight

as he looks at the blocks.

Floppy points to his soft ears.

"Step one: **Stop**," said Floppy.

Bruno stops and looks at

Floppy's face and floppy ears.

Papa Bear takes a deep breath.

"Step two: **Breathe**," said Papa Bear.

Bruno **breathes in and out slowly**

with Papa Bear beside him.

Mama Bear kneels low.

"Step three: **Try again**," said Mama Bear.

Bruno picks up a green block

and **smiles** at Mama Bear.

Floppy claps his paws.

"You **can do it**," said Floppy.

Bruno stacks a blue block

on the green one **carefully**.

Papa Bear nods and watches the tower grow.

Bruno sets a yellow block on top.

The tower **stands tall**

under the warm lamp light.

Mama Bear hugs Bruno.

"You **did it**," said Mama Bear.

Bruno hugs Mama Bear back

and **laughs happily.**

Floppy pats Bruno's arm.

Papa Bear smiles wide.

Bruno says, **"Today is good,"**

and the family sits together

by the warm fire.

The End

About the Author

Nora Gracie Foster is a children's author who loves turning everyday moments into magical adventures. Inspired by the beauty of Canada and the vibrant culture of Belize, she writes playful stories that spark curiosity, laughter, and a love for reading.

Her books are created for curious young readers (ages 3–12) and the grown-ups who read with them — combining imagination, learning, and lots of heart.

Nora believes that storytelling is a superpower — and every page is a chance to explore something new.

 Want to stay in touch or discover more fun adventures?
Look for her cheerful pencil mascot throughout her books!

 # Thank you

We hope you and your little one enjoyed the heartfelt journey of **Bruno's Big Feelings.**

If this story brought comfort, connection, or a little extra calm to your day, **please consider leaving a quick review** on Amazon.

Your kind words help other families discover the book and support children as they learn to manage big emotions with gentle steps.

Just scan below to share your thoughts — it only takes a moment, but it means so much.

♥ With gratitude,

Nora Gracie Foster

Children's Book Author

www.ingramcontent.com/pod-product-compliance
Lightning Source LLC
Chambersburg PA
CBHW042052050526
44107CB00109B/1079